# 7 Steps to Success

## For the Entrepreneur

Dr. Joy Lough

# 7 STEPS TO SUCCESS
## FOR THE ENTREPRENEUR

*DR. JOY LOUGH*

JOY LOUGH
ENTERPRISES

First Printing: 2018

ISBN 978-0-9960656-1-0

Joy Lough Enterprises, LLC
1183 University Dr. #105-125

Burlington, NC 27215

www.joylough.com  910.390.276

# DEDICATION

To entrepreneurs in any stage of their journey, whether you are a startup company, or have been in business for years. I hope that you find this book informative and that it will help you in your journey, both now and in the future.

# CONTENTS

## ACKNOWLEDGMENTS

Special acknowledgment to anyone who ever offered me a kind word of encouragement during this life-changing endeavor. Thank you for pushing me to move forward. And finally, thank you to all the research participants, students, clients and entrepreneurs - without you, neither the journey nor the experience would have been possible.

# DISCLAIMER

The information shared in this book, is the result of research and from my personal interactions with clients/customers. Please understand that I am not in any way suggesting that if you follow these steps that you are guaranteed success in your business venture. Your personal results will vary and depend upon many additional factors including, but not limited to, your background, experience, and work ethic. With any business there are risks, but also keep in mind that there needs to be action and effort on your part for you to realize success.

# INTRODUCTION

When I was working on my PhD, I decided to research success factors for African American entrepreneurs in North Carolina. The research suggested that success factors included goals, mentors, education and knowledge, financial resources, timing, and fear of failure. As a professor who teaches business and works with small business owners/entrepreneurs, I thought it pertinent that I continue to equip myself with tools to help both my students and clients.

I considered conducting research on personality traits but there are so many career assessments and personality tests to determine if there is a good "fit" for a particular position or career. I wanted to delve deeper. I chose to conduct interviews, speaking one-on-one with participants about their entrepreneurial journeys. I asked them questions such as: What worked in their business? Why did it work? What didn't work and why? What do they wish they had known sooner? What would they do differently now? What was the most impactful moment in their entrepreneurial careers? Why?

Even though the original study was conducted in North Carolina, I am sure that entrepreneurs of all races, ages, and regions will find this information helpful in their business or career at any stage of their journey.

I have come to the realization that success factors for entrepreneurs can also transfer over to success in your personal and professional life. Think about it. Other research states that personality traits can be factors for success. Certain personalities excel in particular environments. Certain education degrees or certificates can help you gain a competitive advantage over your peers. The same goes for your entrepreneurial venture. There are several success factors that can contribute to your overall success. Once you are aware of and understand these success factors, then you and your company can become better equipped to face challenges and competition.

The entrepreneurial journey you will take in *7 Steps to Success*, offers no guarantee for success. These are, however, steps that may be taken to improve the chances for success. Most of the clients, with whom I have conferred in the past, shared that these actions helped them.

Some of the steps that are discussed in this book include: Identifying your 3 Ps, Developing Successful Relationships, Education Matters, Timing, Finances, and Goal Setting. I will also share personal experiences, as well as findings from my dissertation research.

*7 Steps to Success* is an "action" book, so I encourage you to take the time to really think about your answers and fill in the blank spaces. It is okay to change your mind. Feel free to go back and make revisions as needed. Remember the process of growing and building your business is ongoing - always. Time is a constant change and there may be circumstances that will force you to make needed adjustments. And that is okay, too.

Yes, I will discuss seven steps, but keep in mind there are others. All seven of these strategies may not resonate with you at the moment, but you will find that all the steps are essential for the start-up stages of your business. Be sure to review each step periodically as your business continues to develop.

Also, while reading look for the links for a free business plan template, a free marketing plan template and link to sign up for the7 Steps to Success Course.

Are you ready?

Let's begin.

# STEP 1: START HERE

You are here. You are reading this book. So now what? Well, let me ask you this:

What does success mean to you?

I have asked the same question to myself and to other business owners and entrepreneurs. Surprisingly, it was not just the money or financial part that equated to success for them or for myself. For most, success is the flexibility spend time with family or to work on other projects. Success is making a difference in someone's life, even if only a few people. Success is being able to pass the three-year mark (since many companies fail within the first three years). Success is being a mentor or role model for others. Success is staying out of the red the first year and then for all the years that follow. Success is being able to live out the passion for business. Imagine that!

Yes, there were times when money did come up in my conversations with entrepreneurs. But money was simply a bonus and was NOT the MAIN definition of success for the participants of my study or for my clients.

Now, with that said, I really do believe that success is a definition that you have to determine for yourself. Success comes in many different forms. No one can tell you about your success or how to measure it. And success may not have just one definition for you. Success can have multiple aspects. Do not limit yourself to what you believe others think your success should be.

**Step 1: Take a few moments and respond to the following questions:**

As a start-up, when you think about your business, what does success look like for you? What does success mean to you? Why?

If you have been in business for a while, think back to when you first started your venture, what did you envision your successful point to be? At what point did you say, "I am successful now!" Not that you should quit once you reach that point, but what defines that milestone for you?

_____

_____

_____

_____

_____

_____

_____

_____

# STEP 2: IDENTIFY YOUR THREE P'S: PASSION, PURPOSE, AND POSSIBILITY

I share with my clients all the time that it is pertinent that you identify your three P's:

## *PASSION,*

## *PURPOSE. and*

## *believing in what is POSSIBLE.*

The first part of Step 2 is for you to figure out what is important to you. What is that one thing that you would do even if you were not paid to do it? You might say that that one passion is a hobby. That may be true, but who says your hobby cannot make you some money? Or impact someone's life?

There is a saying I have heard many times over the years. Find your passion and it will become your purpose. It was hard for me to imagine how that could be a true idea at first. Then, one day, circumstances just fell into place. Allow me to share my story.

I love to write poetry and I kept a journal for years. Actually, I still have poems from when I was 12 years old. I read them from time to time to reminisce. And smile. And get angry. And laugh. And cry. But I also grow. As I realized through my poetry how my life had developed, I felt accomplished. I felt proud. I reminded myself that whatever happened in the past has helped define who I am today. Today I am wiser; I am stronger.

One day, my daughter, being the curious little angel that she was, found my journal. She read a few poems, looked up to me with her beautiful brown eyes, and said, "Why don't you make a book, Mommy?" I laughed at first. But then I thought, "Why not?" So, I did. And my first book, *Tears of Joy: A Poetic Journey in the Life of Ms. Joy*, was born.

The book opened so many doors for me. I started speaking at schools for National Poetry month. Then I performed at a few open mic evenings at local establishments. I was asked to speak at churches, colleges, and community events. The list goes on.

I realized that through my speaking, I transformed lives. I challenged the "normal" ways of thinking. I motivated my listeners. I taught them. Sharing my story freed women from abusive relationships, and it encouraged single mothers to go back to school and stop waiting for that "right time." My stories started the healing process for so many.

I found my passion and it was POETRY!

Poetry led me to my purpose which was to plant seeds, words of wisdom and encouragement, in others. I was able to continue to nourish the seeds through speaking and coaching. I facilitated workshops and invited women to small group sessions where we delved deeper into their situations and mapped out plans to move forward.

And oh, the possibilities! I believed in the possibilities then and still believe in the possibilities today. Following the road of my passion for poetry led me to the place I am today. I am now the author of five books and you are holding the most recent one at this moment. I co-authored my fourth book, and it became a bestseller! I believe there is still more to come. And I am super excited to see what is next!

**Step 2: Respond to the following questions:**

What are you passionate about?  Why?

_____

_____

_____

_____

_____

_____

_____

_____

_____

_____

_____

_____

Once you have found your passion, how does that
help you?  How does that help others?

_____

_____

_____

_____

_____

_____

_____

_____

_____

_____

What is your impactful moment? What is that moment in time when you felt like, "This really matters," and I like who I am now or I love who I have become? This is what I am good at and what I want to continue to do. Keep in mind that it may not be just one moment but a few. In the beginning, I helped women in abusive relationships, but now I am helping entrepreneurs. The underlying theme of my impact is that I am HELPING others. Once you find that theme for you…This is your purpose.

_____

_____

_____

_____

_____

_____

_____

_____

_____

_____

_____

_____

_____

_____

_____

What is your vision for three months from now?
Don't focus on any challenges or obstacles. Don't
worry about the "what ifs." Don't give a second
thought to what others may think. If you have
someone who encourages you, that is wonderful. But
do not let what that person says or does impact your
focus in a negative way. Take pictures. Draw it - if the
words are hard to find.

What is your vision for six months from now?

_____

_____

_____

_____

_____

_____

_____

_____

_____

_____

_____

_____

_____

_____

A year from now?

_____

_____

_____

_____

_____

_____

_____

_____

_____

_____

_____

_____

_____

Five years from now?

_____

_____

_____

_____

_____

_____

_____

_____

_____

_____

_____

_____

Everything you have listed is your possibility!

The next page is intentionally left blank. Use it to draw your vision! Write your vision. Tear it out and stick it in a place you will see every day (your bathroom mirror or your refrigerator, for example).

# STEP 3: DEVELOP SUCCESSFUL RELATIONSHIPS

So, my next question to you is. . .

## Do you have a mentor?

Do you have someone to confide in that will be loyal to you? I share with all my clients that it is very important to have that "person." Someone you can bounce ideas off of and who will be honest with you. Someone who may have already been where you are trying to go.

## Do you really even need a mentor?

I am sure you have heard the saying that a client who represents himself in court has a fool for a lawyer. Think about it. No one person can do EVERYTHING on his or her own. We all need help in some way or another. I tell my children often "No matter how many degrees you have, you will never know everything." That is why I continue my education and stay around people who can feed knowledge to me and my life.

Do you remember times when you were in school or even at work and you were put into teams? It was a better way to get ideas from or bounce ideas off of others. There may have been an item or thought that you alone might have missed, but others in the group were able to catch. Teamwork helps in problem solving. Teams also help people use their strengths versus being forced to do something that is not beneficial to an idea or plan. And working in teams helps save time, especially if there are deadlines.

Why not have someone on your team to help guide you, support you, or be your cheerleader? That's what a mentor does. If you have ever played a sport or an instrument, it was always a good feeling to look out into the crowd during a competition or concert and see someone you knew. They realized how much time and effort you put in to practicing and developing your technique. They watched you grow from knowing very little to the place you were then, singing, playing a solo, or becoming the star player of the team. That is what a mentor does.

A mentor is not always easy to find, but think about this: do you have someone in your life who you can count on now to support you? When you gave a presentation in the past at a community event, or implemented a project at church or work, who came to cheer you on?

Who were the first people you told about your desire to start your entrepreneurial venture? These people can be your mentors, and if not, they can surely be a part of your support team.

You have heard the saying that it takes a village. The same rule applies for your entrepreneurial ventures. I will say it again; no one can do it ALL alone. You may be able to complete some tasks in a business, like making a website and even starting the business plan. But can you also complete the business plan, get new clients, organize the day-to-day service for the clients, build whatever gadget you have invented, and still have time for a mental break? One person may be really good at one area, but that same person cannot do it all by him or herself – at least not with total efficiency.

Allow me to share a story about my friend. Let's call her Sally Sue. Sally has a consulting company similar to mine. She also has over 20 years of experience. I met her at a networking event, and we started talking about our businesses. It was then that we discovered how much we had in common. After a few additional meetings, I asked her if she would be my mentor. I chose Sally because I admired her and what she did to help others in the community. She has offered me guidance for over four years. I am thankful that she reminds me to take time out for myself. She tells me when I need to say "no" to clients who are not consistent in their follow-through or who want constant advice for free. It is okay to share ideas or advice at times but not on a daily basis. She offers motivation and a listening ear when I need to vent.

My grandmother always said, "Watch the company you keep." Do you know why she said this? One main reason is because, "You are an average of the five people you hang around the most." (Jim Rohn) I believe my grandmother saw how at times I was naïve and did not see how people took advantage of my skills or kindness. I know my grandmother wanted me to understand my value. She did not want me to be around someone who did not appreciate me or my talents. She wanted me to own who I am and what contribution I am making or giving to others. She wanted me to be in give-and-take relationships. So, with my grandmother's words in mind, why not be around someone who is going to uplift you, motivate you, encourage you, teach you, and lead you?

This is not a journey to be traveled alone. Find that someone or those persons who will be a part of your village or team so that you can grow. Hopefully, you will be able to continue to add to your knowledge of what to do and what not to do as it relates to your business. A mentor will help you reach short and long-term goals. A mentor will help you make your vision a reality.

## Step 3: Respond to the following questions:

Who can you reach out to for help or assistance?
Who are the people in your "village?" Why did you
choose them? What characteristics do they have that
can help you in your journey?

_____

_____

_____

_____

_____

_____

_____

_____

_____

_____

_____

_____

_____

If you cannot think of anyone right off, consider these questions. How often do you network? If you do not or don't often interact with others, then there is no better time than the present. Join a club. Go to an event that interests you. Search and find an event on Facebook that would be a great networking opportunity. Ask around - maybe someone knows of an event that is not posted.

_____

_____

_____

_____

_____

_____

_____

_____

_____

_____

_____

Are you on Linkedin? Is there someone who has similar aspirations as you? How is their business going? Is it evident that they are striving for success? Why not reach out to them?

_____

_____

_____

_____

_____

_____

_____

_____

_____

_____

_____

_____

_____

Are you in Facebook groups that are not just time wasters? Why? Who in the group can help?

_____

_____

_____

_____

_____

_____

_____

_____

_____

_____

_____

_____

_____

_____

_____

_____

_____

Have you "liked" and subscribed to pages that will help you with your short and long-term goals? If so, what are they? List the sites here:

_____

_____

_____

_____

_____

_____

_____

_____

_____

_____

_____

_____

_____

What about blogs from influencers? Have you
subscribed to any? List them here.

_____

_____

_____

_____

_____

_____

_____

_____

_____

_____

_____

_____

_____

Why not create your own group on a social media platform? Outline your ideas and strategies here.

_____

_____

_____

_____

_____

_____

_____

_____

_____

_____

_____

_____

_____

_____

Are you involved in the community? Are you a
member of any organizations? Non-profit boards?
List opportunities to volunteer or connect here.

_____

_____

_____

_____

_____

_____

_____

_____

_____

_____

_____

_____

_____

List companies or organizations doing something similar to what you do. Is there someone you know already working there? If not, contact someone in the marketing department or public relations to see how you can help or volunteer.

_____

_____

_____

_____

_____

_____

_____

_____

_____

_____

_____

_____

_____

# STEP 4: EDUCATION MATTERS

I have been asked the following question countless times: "Do you need multiple degrees for success?"

Another question that is common is, "Does education even matter?" Well, that depends. If you are delving into a venture that is foreign to you, then you may need to read up on what all is involved.

My response to these questions is the same. Having a degree is not mandatory to be successful. But I do encourage my students and clients to take some financial classes and a few Business Management, Human Resources, or Marketing classes. I personally offer classes periodically during the year, also. (There is more information about these resources at the end of this book.)

You do not necessarily need to have a master's degree in any particular subject because we all know that there are many successful entrepreneurs who do not even have a high school diploma. Therefore, a college education may not even be a benefit in your particular field. But I have talked to some bank financers who provide small business loans. They believe that having some sort of education, even if it is an associate degree, shows dedication and fortitude. It is this type of dedication that may be the deciding factor in whether or not you receive a business loan.

Financial classes will help you understand the fiscal matters in a business. These classes can help you answer questions such as: What is a debit or a credit? What happens if you choose to offer credit to your customers? What taxes are you responsible for? Why? Does the type of entity have anything to do with the amount of money you can make?

I encourage clients to take business classes because many investors require a business plan or marketing plan. Keep in mind that this plan is simply a tool to help you see where you are now and where you want to be in the future.

**Did you know that Joy Lough Enterprises, LLC has a business plan template for free? Get yours at bit.ly/jlebizplan**

**Get your marketing plan here bit.ly/jlemarketing**

I encourage clients to take a Human Resources class because it helps them to understand people and personalities. You are oftentimes able to take courses that deal with conflict resolution and training. Having these skills can help when dealing with the public, even if you work on a solo basis. If you have an irate customer, you want to have the skills to calm them down and still close the deal. You may have an undecided patron; you want to be able to have a conversation to figure out what package will work best for them. You may have an error in data that caused you to overcharge or undercharge for an item or service. Knowing how to combat issues is key to retaining clients. All these subjects and topics are essential for a company, even as they are ready to hire their first employee.

The conflict may not be with a customer – sometimes problems occur between employees. Being equipped with skills or training such as a human resource management course will allow you to make more informed decisions as to how to move forward in certain situations regarding employees, volunteers, or interns. Managing people is not always an easy task.

I offer Leadership and Human Resources workshops. **For more information go here:**

 **bit.ly/jleworkshops**

**When you are ready to hire, here is an Onboarding checklist to help**

**bit.ly/jlechecklist**

## Step 4: Respond to the following questions:

What are some local community colleges, colleges, or universities in your area? What classes can you take to help manage your business? Did you know that Joy Lough Enterprises offers classes to help with the start-up and development of your business too? More information is provided at the end of the book.

_____

_____

_____

_____

_____

_____

_____

_____

_____

_____

What classes are you passionate about? How can they help you and your business? Let's say you want to venture into photography. Could an art class be beneficial right now? Or perhaps you want to be a secretary or virtual assistance. Can a Microsoft certification help you?

_____

_____

_____

_____

_____

_____

_____

_____

_____

_____

_____

_____

_____

# STEP 5: LET'S TALK ABOUT MONEY

I have been asked questions like, "Do you need to be rich or have been born with a silver spoon in your mouth in order to make it in a business?" No, but you do need to know about finances and financial resources. Having financial knowledge is an important aspect of starting and continuing a business.

Did you know that there are many opportunities to start a business venture for less than $100? Listed below are some examples of businesses that you can start with the equipment you may already have at home. You will only need a computer and internet service to get started.

**A Virtual Assistant:** Do you have strong organizational skills? Are you good at time management? Do you have excellent communication skills? If so, these skills can be just what you need to gain your first client.

**Social Media Consultant:** Do you love Facebook? Twitter? Instagram? Do you have an impressive following? When companies or people look for assistance to grow their following, then seeing what you accomplished is the best testimonial you can share.

**A Website Developer:** Are you creative? Do you have knowledge of feedback forms, shopping carts, or service pages? These are some of the skills needed to help develop websites. With the number of templates available, there is an opportunity to build a clientele with your knowledge.

If your goal is to keep a few clients and not grow to full scale with your business, then finances may not be much of a concern for you.

But if your goal is to have 100 or more clients within a year or two then, the mindset needs to change. With 100 or more clients, you need to move into a physical location, rather than work from home. You need additional computers, more desks, telephones, business cards, signs, additional personnel, and the list goes on. How do finances play a part now?

Without a financial background, knowledge about credit for you and your business, or how to budget properly, then money issues can make or break your business. It is essential to be aware and knowledgeable of these complications as your business grows.

Other matters to consider are: Am I charging what I am worth? Do I make enough to cover my basic essentials such as utilities, internet, or rent?

**For Step 5: Respond to the following questions:**

What is your price list? (You may need additional space here.)

_____

_____

_____

_____

_____

_____

_____

_____

Did you research the costs to ensure that you are competitive, will make money, and will not go into the red (negative)?

_____

_____

_____

_____

_____

_____

_____

_____

_____

_____

_____

_____

What is the lifestyle you want to lead?

_____

_____

_____

_____

_____

_____

Once you answer these essential components, then you can answer the next few financial questions: How much will this venture cost you? What is your budget? What can you afford to spend/invest of your personal finances?

This point is where the research comes in...Research what others are investing in start-ups similar to yours. Will you need to include everything they are doing right now or can certain items wait a year or two? For instance, if you start a pet-grooming service and plan to only offer services for dogs under 15 pounds, but your research includes dogs up to 40 pounds, then you may not need as many items in your budget.

_____

_____

_____

_____

_____

_____

_____

_____

_____

_____


What else do you need to start your business? How much will it cost? The following is **NOT** a complete list, but it will help get you started.

- **Business Name**
- **Tax ID**
- **Business Structure (LLC, Corporation, Partnership, etc.)**
- **Any Needed Permits, Licenses, Registrations**
- **Accountant:** I advise clients and students to have an accountant who will help with taxes and answer any financial questions they may have.  Again, having some knowledge will help you because even the basics need to be known. But unless you are familiar with all the new laws in your state that can change at any given moment, you do not want your

neighbor's cousin's uncle working on your business taxes!

- **Mentor**: This topic is discussed in Step 3
- **Lawyer:** Consult a lawyer, even if it's Prepaid Legal. You can also contact LegalZoom.
- **Website:** Create a web presence, including social media.
- **Assistant:** Remember, you can always get an intern to start off and offer a stipend rather than have them on the payroll.
- **Marketing Materials**
- **Office Supplies**
- **Location**
- **Phone**
- **Logo**
- **Business Cards**
- **Bank accounts**
- **Trademarks, Patents, Copyrights**

_____

_____

_____

What financial resources are available to me?

- Friends,
- Family
- Banks
- Small Business Administration (SBA)
- Chamber of Commerce
- Other organizations/ community services that support local businesses

_____

_____

_____

_____

_____

_____

_____

_____

_____

_____

_____

I encourage you to **revisit this section often.**

Now list some people that you can contact today (or at least this week to help you get started)

| | |
|---|---|
| Name | |
| Phone # | |
| Email | |
| Date Contacted | |
| Need Follow up? | |
| When | |
| How Much Given/Loaned? | |
| Notes | |

| Name | |
|---|---|
| Phone # | |
| Email | |
| Date Contacted | |
| Need Follow up? | |
| When | |
| How Much Given/Loaned? | |
| Notes | |

| | |
|---|---|
| Name | |
| Phone # | |
| Email | |
| Date Contacted | |
| Need Follow up? | |
| When | |
| How Much Given/Loaned? | |
| Notes | |

| Name | |
|---|---|
| Phone # | |
| Email | |
| Date Contacted | |
| Need Follow up? | |
| When | |
| How Much Given/Loaned? | |
| Notes | |

| Name | |
|---|---|
| Phone # | |
| Email | |
| Date Contacted | |
| Need Follow up? | |
| When | |
| How Much Given/Loaned? | |
| Notes | |

## STEP 6: TIMING

When you are planning to launch a book – you choose a specific date. That date often is due to a number of factors: you completed writing the book, you have the final edits approved by the editor/publisher, you have marketing strategies in place, etc. The same applies to when you plan to launch your entrepreneurial venture. The timing should be planned.

In my dissertation, I asked participants about the timing of their ventures. "How does the time of entry play a part in your success?" I hoped to discover if there was a correlation with the timing of entry and the success of their business ventures. When I received the answers, I realized that this question does not apply to just the time you choose to introduce your venture to the world, but also the time in your life that you have dedicated to introduce your venture.

For example, I have a client that worked full time while trying to start her business. She wished to start a business because circumstances were not as favorable as she would have liked at her full-time job. She desperately wanted to be able to work on her own terms. The issue was that she did not have the funds to step away from her full-time job and devote her full attention to her business venture. Not only were the funds not available, but timing was a factor also. She was a single parent, and the ability to juggle work, the new venture, parenting, and herself became a challenge. Together, we were able to come up with a plan and schedule, so she was able to transition to being full-time at her new business venture. This timing took about a year of planning and sacrifice to make it happen. Through focus and determination, she is now enjoying her success because she actually took the time out to make the right moves.

Keep in mind that organization and time management can play a role when you consider the questions for this step. Sometimes we just need patience.

## Step 6: Respond to the following questions:

Are you currently working full or part-time? If you are working full-time, how much time can you invest in your venture on a weekly basis?

_____

_____

_____

_____

_____

_____

If you work part-time, do you have necessary tools available right now to start your venture and support it properly?

_____

_____

_____

_____

_____

_____

Is this the right time for you to get involved in a business? Why or why not?

_____

_____

_____

_____

_____

_____

_____

If right now isn't the best time, how long do you think you will need? Why?

_____

_____

_____

_____

_____

_____

_____

What is the economy like? Is there a need for your product or service? Have you conducted research to find out?

_____

_____

_____

_____

_____

_____

Do you have what it takes to start now? What are you bringing to the table?

_____

_____

_____

_____

_____

_____

_____

To help you further explore these questions, I want you to delve deeper and conduct a self SWOT analysis. A SWOT will help determine your personal Strengths, Weaknesses, Opportunities and Threats. Sometimes it is good to have a list of what you can do and what you are not able to do. By having this record, you will be better equipped to analyze where you need to seek additional assistance in particular areas.

Complete your Self SWOT below as part of Step 6.

# My Self SWOT

**Strengths:**

List your strengths here. What is that one characteristic that makes you a rock star? What can you do to help your company grow? List your knowledge or background here.

| **Weaknesses:**<br><br>List your weaknesses but do not think of them as a weakness, but rather a chance for improvement. | |
|---|---|

**Opportunities:**

Write down opportunities that you have currently. Are there classes offered at a nearby community college? What about your local library?

Are there any networking events coming up?

**Threats:**

What are some threats to your ability to move forward? How will you address them?

**Example:**
Fear is a Threat

**What will you do**?
Subscribe to a motivation blog.

# STEP 7: JUST MAKE IT HAPPEN

In steps 1 through 6,

1. We discussed the starting point and you. You were asked to take the time to define what success means to you.

2. We talked about identifying your 3 Ps – Passion, Purpose and Possibility.

3. We examined the need for developing successful relationships.

4. We discussed education and business knowledge.

5. We explored finances – the money involved in your business.

6. We considered the timing factor in your venture.

7. For step 7 – we are going to … Just make it happen.

I would like for you to read and respond to the series of questions concerning the topics in each of the following sections.

## Marketing

Once you answer the following questions, I encourage you to continue to do market research in the industry you choose and in the location of where you will start and grow your business.

You may need to get specific here. Remember you have a target market. You may have additional markets that you help or cater to, but there should be a target. For instance, my target market is small businesses in the start-up phase of their ventures. But I also work with clients in other phases, including entrepreneurs who have been in business for 10+ years. Sometimes we revisit steps that are in the startup phase. I also work with individuals. But again, my target is small businesses, because I feel that is where I can help the most with my experience and background in leadership, human resources, management, and entrepreneurship.

Who are your customers/clients? And why are they your clients?

_____

_____

_____

_____

_____

_____

_____

_____

_____

_____

_____

_____

_____

What is the customer's need?  How do your products
or services fill the needs of your customers?

_____

_____

_____

_____

_____

_____

_____

_____

_____

_____

_____

_____

_____

_____

What do you want to share with your clients? In this section, think about your product and/or service and what makes you unique. Talk about how you add value:

_____

_____

_____

_____

_____

_____

_____

_____

_____

_____

_____

_____

_____

Who is your competition? Why are they the
competition?

_____

_____

_____

_____

_____

_____

_____

_____

_____

_____

_____

_____

_____

_____

What makes your business different? Have you conducted any research to support this?

_____

_____

_____

_____

_____

_____

_____

_____

_____

_____

_____

_____

_____

_____

How are you going to market your products/services?

_____

_____

_____

_____

_____

_____

_____

_____

_____

_____

_____

_____

_____

_____

_____

What are some risks or obstacles in your business
venture?

_____

_____

_____

_____

_____

_____

_____

_____

_____

_____

_____

_____

_____

_____

What is your plan to conquer the risks or obstacles that you listed above? Set some goals to make the plan happen.

_____

_____

_____

_____

_____

_____

_____

_____

_____

_____

_____

_____

_____

**Get your marketing plan here bit.ly/jlemarketing**

## Goal Setting

There is a saying "It's ok to change the plan (marketing, strategic, business plan), but never the goal!" If your goal is to leave something for your children or grandchildren, you must remain focused. By being focused and having a plan, you are more likely to have continuity in your business. Maybe your goal is to work in your business venture full time. You may want to have the freedom of working on your own time. In order to achieve any of these milestones in life, setting goals are vital.

I know there are a lot of questions to consider, but I believe it is very important to know **why** you are doing what you are doing. With this intention in mind, you will always know what your end goal is. Remember the definition of success for you. Remember the purpose, passion, and possibilities. Remember the vision you made a drawing about or wrote about. What was your **why** for the answers you gave? Hopefully, you are connecting your why with the information from all the previous chapters by now.

What are some of your long and short-term goals for your business? I encourage you to write them down and keep them in a location where you can periodically view them. Post them on a board or record them in a book or journal. Again, you want to be reminded of your goal and **why** you are doing what you are doing.

What are your top five goals or objectives for your business?

1. _____

   _____

   _____

2. _____

   _____

   _____

3. _____

   _____

   _____

4. _____

_____

_____

5. _____

_____

_____

What is your 30-day goal for your business? It may be as simple as, "Make my first $5,000."

_____

_____

_____

_____

_____

_____

_____

_____

_____

What are the three steps you will take to accomplish this 30-day goal?

1. _____

   _____

   _____

   _____

2. _____

   _____

   _____

   _____

3. _____

   _____

   _____

   _____

What is your 90-day goal for your business? It may be as simple as, "Make my first $75,000."

_____

_____

_____

_____

_____

_____

_____


What are the three steps you will take to accomplish this goal?

1. _____

_____

_____

_____

2. _____

_____

_____

_____

3. _____

_____

_____

_____

What is your one-year goal for your business?

_____

_____

_____

_____

_____

_____

_____

_____

_____

What are the three steps you will take to accomplish this?

1. _____

_____

_____

_____

2. _____

_____

_____

_____

3. _____

_____

_____

_____

Even with these goals in mind, let's break them down even more. Create daily goals to help you reach the first 30, then 60, and then 90 days of your venture.

Choose something daily that will help your business and commit to doing it each day.

Fill out the following To-Do List each day. You may not complete all seven blanks – and that's okay, for now. Just keep doing useful tasks daily to grow your business.

| Sunday | |
|---|---|
| | 1. _____ |
| | 2. _____ |
| | 3. _____ |
| | 4. _____ |
| | 5. _____ |
| | 6. _____ |
| | 7. _____ |

| Monday | |
|---|---|
| | 1. _____ |
| | 2. _____ |
| | 3. _____ |
| | 4. _____ |
| | 5. _____ |
| | 6. _____ |
| | 7. _____ |
| Tuesday | |
| | 1. _____ |
| | 2. _____ |
| | 3. _____ |
| | 4. _____ |
| | 5. _____ |
| | 6. _____ |
| | 7. _____ |

| Wednesday | |
| --- | --- |
| | 1. _____ |
| | 2. _____ |
| | 3. _____ |
| | 4. _____ |
| | 5. _____ |
| | 6. _____ |
| | 7. _____ |
| Thursday | |
| | 1. _____ |
| | 2. _____ |
| | 3. _____ |
| | 4. _____ |
| | 5. _____ |
| | 6. _____ |
| | 7. _____ |

| Friday | |
|---|---|
| | 1. _____ |
| | 2. _____ |
| | 3. _____ |
| | 4. _____ |
| | 5. _____ |
| | 6. _____ |
| | 7. _____ |
| Saturday | |
| | 1. _____ |
| | 2. _____ |
| | 3. _____ |
| | 4. _____ |
| | 5. _____ |
| | 6. _____ |
| | 7. _____ |

Now I challenge you to do something daily to help you **STAY MOTIVATED** to complete your daily goals!  Even if you have to start off with 3 goals, then move on to 5, and then 7… do that.

Just make it happen!

If you need help or want additional assistance, I encourage you to visit my website www.joylough.com Connect with me on Facebook www.facebook.com/joylough.

LinkedIn

www.linkedin.com/in/joylough

Twitter

www.twitter.com/joylough

Instagram

www.instagram.com/joylough

There is an upcoming four-week masterclass to further help you with your entrepreneurial journey. If you want additional information – please go here.

Bit.ly/jle7stepsclass

**HERE'S TO YOUR SUCCESS!**

# ABOUT THE AUTHOR

**Joy Lough, PhD** is an Author and Small Business Start-up Strategist. With over 20 years of experience in entrepreneurship, business, and human resources, she is the CEO of Joy Lough Enterprises, LLC. Her mission is to IMPACT lives professionally and personally through education, motivation, and inspiration.

Dr. Joy is passionate about helping build and foster productive and prosperous members of society. Dr. Joy has spoken and lectured at schools, colleges, universities, churches, and community events in a variety of venues.

For booking or more information contact:
info@joylough.com  910.390.2765  www.joylough.com

Make sure you subscribe connect with Dr. Joy to get updates on giveaways, classes, and other events.

www.ingramcontent.com/pod-product-compliance
Lightning Source LLC
Chambersburg PA
CBHW060629210326
41520CB00010B/1530